I0824596

Tiger
Maria Koran and
John Willis
EYEDISCOVER

Go to **www.eyediscover.com** and enter this book's unique code.

BOOK CODE

AVA26969

EYEDISCOVER brings you optic readalongs that support active learning.

Published by AV2
276 5th Avenue, Suite 704 #917
New York, NY 10001
Website: www.eyediscover.com

Library of Congress Control Number: 2021937106

ISBN 978-1-7911-3996-4 (hardcover)

Printed in Guangzhou, China
1 2 3 4 5 6 7 8 9 0 25 24 23 22 21

042021
102120

Project Coordinator: John Willis
Designer: Mandy Christiansen

The publisher acknowledges Getty Images, Alamy, Shutterstock, and Minden Pictures as the primary image suppliers for this title.

EYEDISCOVER provides enriched content, optimized for tablet use, that supplements and complements this book. EYEDISCOVER books strive to create inspired learning and engage young minds in a total learning experience.

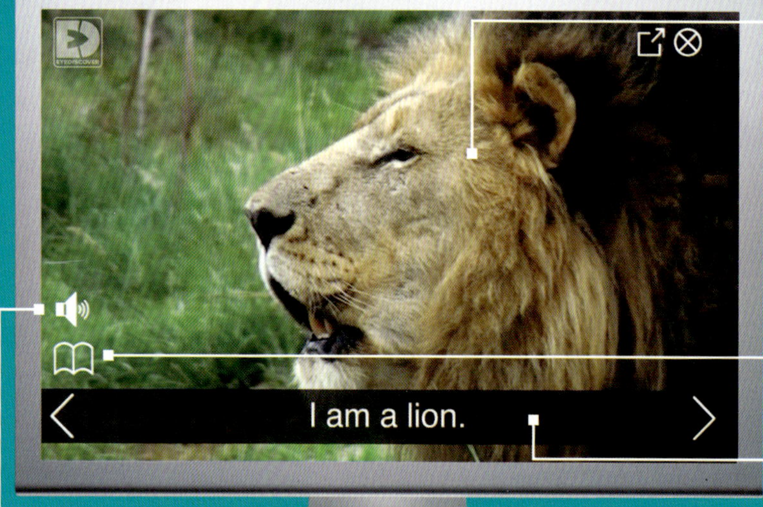

Watch
Video content brings each page to life.

Browse
Thumbnails make navigation simple.

Read
Follow along with text on the screen.

Listen
Hear each page read aloud.

Your EYEDISCOVER Optic Readalongs come alive with...

Audio
Listen to the entire book read aloud.

Video
High resolution videos turn each spread into an optic readalong.

OPTIMIZED FOR
- ✓ TABLETS
- ✓ WHITEBOARDS
- ✓ COMPUTERS
- ✓ AND MUCH MORE!

This title is part of our EyeDiscover digital subscription

1-Year EyeDiscover Subscription
ISBN 978-1-4896-8346-5

Access all EyeDiscover titles with our digital subscription.
Sign up for a FREE trial at **www.eyediscover.com/trial**

Tiger
In this book, you will learn about
• what it is
• what it looks like
• how it lives
and much more!

Tigers are known for their size. They are the world's largest cats.

Tigers only eat meat. A tiger's striped fur helps it sneak up on the animals it eats.

Tigers usually hunt at night. They see well in the dark.

Tigers are fast animals. They can run as fast as a car.

Tigers are very good swimmers. They often spend time in water.

Tigers are quiet. They cannot purr and do not often roar.

A baby tiger is called a cub. A tiger mother usually has two to four cubs at a time.

Young tigers live with their mothers. A group of tigers is called an ambush.

No two tigers have the same stripes. People used to hunt tigers for their striped coats.

A **Siberian tiger** can grow **up to 13 feet** (4 meters) **long**.

Most countries **BANNED** tiger hunting in the **1970s**.

TIGERS can live in **temperatures** as low as **-40°** Fahrenheit (–40° Celsius).

There are **6 different** kinds of tigers living today.

A **TIGER'S CLAWS** can be **4 inches** (10 centimeters) **long.**

KEY WORDS

Research has shown that as much as 65 percent of all written material published in English is made up of 300 words. These 300 words cannot be taught using pictures or learned by sounding them out. They must be recognized by sight. This book contains 47 common sight words to help young readers improve their reading fluency and comprehension. This book also teaches young readers several important content words, such as proper nouns. These words are paired with pictures to aid in learning and improve understanding.

Page	Sight Words First Appearance
4	are, for, the, their, they, world
7	a, animals, eat, helps, it, on, only, up
8	at, in, night, see, well
11	as, can, car, run
12	good, often, time, very, water
15	and, do, not
16	four, has, is, mother, to, two
19	an, group, live, of, with, young
20	have, no, people, same

Page	Content Words First Appearance
4	cats, size, tigers
7	fur, meat
8	dark
12	swimmers
15	purr, roar
16	cub
19	ambush
20	coats, stripes

Watch
Video content brings each page to life.

Browse
Thumbnails make navigation simple.

Read
Follow along with text on the screen.

Listen
Hear each page read aloud.

Go to www.eyediscover.com and enter this book's unique code.

BOOK CODE

AVA26969